Desmond goes Boating

by Althea
illustrated by the author

brary of Congress Cataloging in Publication Data

thea.
Desmond goes boating.

SUMMARY: Desmond and Mrs. Chubb spend the ternoon boating on a nearby lake.
[1. Boats and boating—Fiction. 2. Dinosaurs—ction] I. Title.
7.A4638Ddf 1981 [E] 80-39857
BN 0-86625-101-4

Rourke Publications, Inc.
Windermere, Florida

Mrs. Chubb was going to the park for the day. She asked Desmond if he would like to go with her.

Desmond said that
would be great fun.
"Can I give you a lift,
Mrs. Chubb?" he asked.

"Thank you, that would be kind," she said.
So they set off on their adventure.

Mrs. Chubb brought a picnic basket.
Desmond wondered what was in it.

There was a big lake in the park.
"Can we go out in a boat?"
asked Desmond.

"Later, after we have had our lunch,"
said Mrs. Chubb.
"Let us sit here under the trees.
We can watch the people."

After they had eaten their lunch
Desmond played soccer.

The ball got stuck in a tree.
But, Desmond soon rescued it.

"Come along.
We will rent one of those long boats.
We can go out on the lake,"
said Mrs. Chubb.

They paid their money.
The man let them have
his biggest long boat.
Desmond just fit in it.

Mrs. Chubb was good at boating.
They were soon out
in the middle of the lake.

Desmond felt very happy.

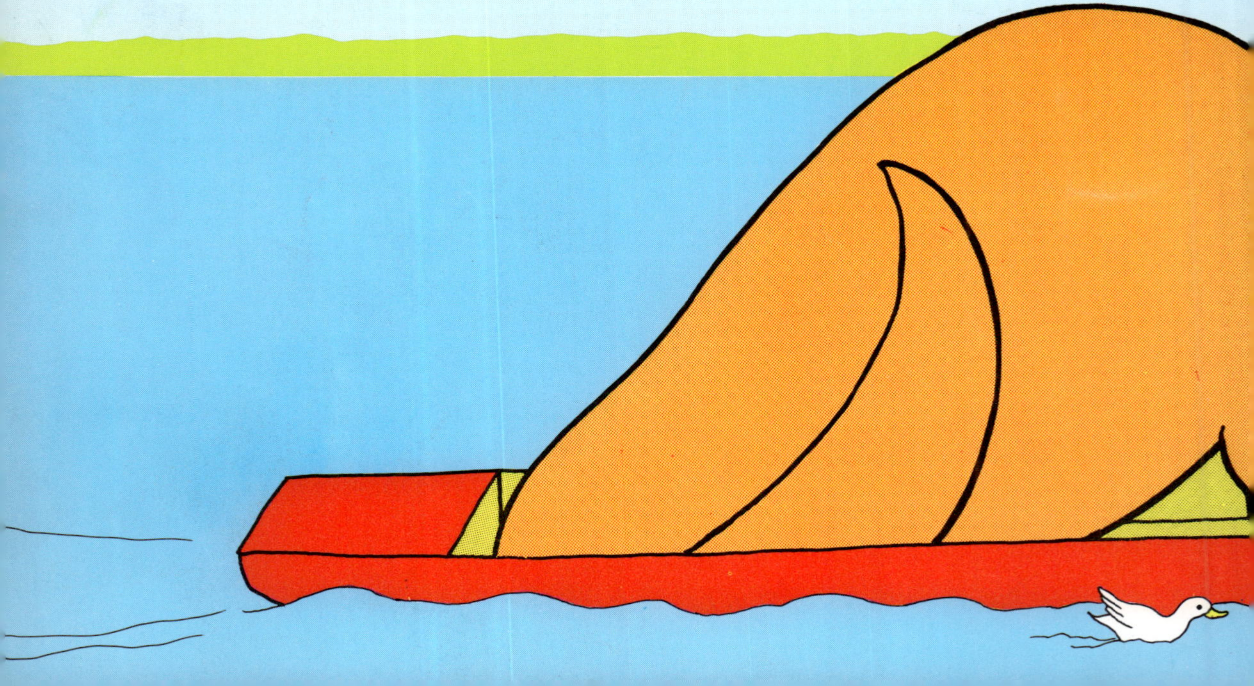

They had some bread left over from lunch.
They threw it into the water.
Then, they watched as the ducks
raced to get it.

Suddenly, the pole stuck in the mud.
Mrs. Chubb held on to it.
But, the boat floated away
without her.

"Help! This is terrible!"
cried Mrs. Chubb.
"What shall I do?
Help me!"

Desmond thought for a moment.

"Do not worry," he said.
"I think I can move the boat
with my tail."

The boat rocked as Desmond put his tail into the water.

Mrs. Chubb held on to the pole tightly.
"Hurry up," she cried.
"I cannot hold on much longer."

Desmond paddled the boat to her.
He was just in time to save Mrs. Chubb.
She almost fell into the water.

"Oh! Thank goodness you saved me, Desmond," she said.

When the people in the park
saw Desmond save Mrs. Chubb
they all cheered.

Desmond rather liked paddling.
The water was not too cold.
Everybody wanted to have
a ride in his boat.

At last they had to
take the boat back.

The boat man said,
"You can have a free ride
whenever you like.
You get me lots of customers."

"That was an exciting day," said Desmond as they went home.

"A bit too exciting for me!" laughed Mrs. Chubb.